# NEWSPAPER

## F · U · N

**Activities for Young Children**

by Bobbye S. Goldstein and Gabriel F. Goldstein

**FEARON TEACHER AIDS**

Simon & Schuster Supplementary Education Group

Copyeditors: Lisa Schwimmer and Kristin Eclov
Illustration: Corbin Hillam
Design: Diann Abbott
Cover Design: Marek-Janci Design

ISBN 0-86653-967-0

Printed in the United States of America
1. 9 8 7 6 5 4 3 2 1

# About the Authors

Bobbye S. Goldstein is a popular speaker and writer both nationally and internationally on a variety of subjects related to reading. A major portion of her career was spent as a reading specialist with the New York City Board of Education. She is a former Board Member of the International Reading Association and a Past President of the Manhattan Council. Bobbye was a founder of the renowned annual Parents and Reading Conference sponsored by the Manhattan Council in cooperation with Fordham University at Lincoln Center and served as co-director of two of Fordham University's summer institutes. She is the recipient of the prestigious International Reading Association's Special Service Award and was honored by Reading Is Fundamental with their Distinguished Volunteer Service Award. Her first book, *Bear in Mind: A Book of Bear Poems,* was an American Booksellers' Association Pick of the List. Her second book, *What's on the Menu?,* is a recently published book of food poems. Her latest book is *Inner Chimes: Poems on Poetry*. Bobbye lives in New York City with her husband, Gabe.

Gabriel F. Goldstein's interest in newspapers dates back to his college days when he was business manager of New York University's Washington Square College Bulletin. A chemist by profession, Gabe worked for Interchemical Corporation (subsequently known as Inmont Corporation), a large manufacturer of inks and coatings. In the course of his career, he developed a unique set of inks for printing on plastic film for which he was awarded several patents. He traveled around the United States and Canada, as well as England, helping with the marketing of the company's products, including many of which he developed. He was a contributor to Chemical Abstracts, wrote articles for technical magazines, and spoke at professional meetings. After retiring from United Technologies, Inc. (successor to Inmont Corporation), he joined his wife in literacy efforts. Gabe lives with his wife, Bobbye, in New York City.

*For Dr. Betty Sullivan and Ruth Finn, friends from NIE (Newspapers in Education).*

*Bobbye S. Goldstein*
*and*
*Gabriel F. Goldstein*

# Contents

# Introduction

Newspapers are a readily available and inexpensive source of material for a multitude of activities which help children become more capable readers and writers. Newspapers inform, educate, and entertain. However, their use in home and school programs for young children has not been fully maximized.

*Newspaper Fun: Activities for Young Children* offers practical suggestions for meaningful ways to use this great resource. The activities in this book are presented in an organized fashion, ranging from the simplest to the more difficult. Since repetition and reinforcement are important in the learning experience of children, some ideas are variations on a specific theme.

We recommend working on only one activity at a time. Young children work best on a project for no more than an hour or so. Discontinue any activity before children become restless. Reading and writing should be an enjoyable experience both for the children and for those working with them. The projects in this book are suitable for individual as well as group instruction. One last note: Remember, young children's activities should always be supervised.

Bobbye S. Goldstein
Gabriel F. Goldstein

# GETTING STARTED

# Tear Pictures

## Materials

- ■ newspaper
- ■ paste
- ■ construction paper
- ■ white chalk or crayon

One of the simplest things to do with newspapers is to tear them. Give children sheets of newspaper to tear into various shapes. These free-form shapes can then be mounted on construction paper. Black paper provides an especially effective background. Print the children's names on their work with white chalk or crayon.

Both tearing and pasting use large and small muscles and help children prepare for later cutting and writing skills.

# Learning to Use a Blunt-Edge Scissors

## Materials

- classified section of the newspaper
- blunt-edge scissors
- paste
- crayons

*Note: Young children should only be given a blunt-edge scissors. These can be obtained at toy and school-supply stores.*

The classified section of the newspaper is particularly useful for cutting and writing activities because this section has clearly defined columns and lines. Cutting with a scissors follows the tearing process and is a forerunner of scribbling and writing.

Have children cut the paper on the dark lines separating the columns on the classified page. The resulting strips can be rolled to form circles and made into long chains for festive occasions. The strips can be colored with different crayons appropriate to specific holidays.

# Learning to Write and Draw on the Lines

## Materials

- classified section of the newspaper
- thick crayons
- wide felt markers

**T**urn the classified page of the paper to a horizontal position. If the line dividers of the columns are too light, darken them with a felt-tip marker. The wide columns provide space where children can learn to stay within boundaries as they write or draw. In order to give the children plenty of room for this activity, spread the newspaper on the floor and have the children work there. Thick crayons and wide felt markers are preferable. Thin crayons break very easily. This project will help the children learn to stay on the lines, which will be useful later when they start formal handwriting.

# Coloring Holiday Pictures

## Materials

- ■ newspaper
- ■ blunt-edge scissors
- ■ crayons
- ■ construction paper
- ■ paste

**T**hroughout the year, especially at holiday times and other special occasions, newspapers have many pictures the children can cut out and color. Once colored, the children's pictures may be mounted on construction paper and displayed in the classroom or at home.

Keep a cumulative file of appropriate pictures when you see them. They can come in handy on a rainy day.

# Stained-Glass Windows

## Materials

- newspaper
- black felt marker
- crayons
- black construction paper
- paste

Fold pieces of the newspaper into square or rectangular shapes. With a black felt marker, draw random lines on the newspaper to create a stained glass appearance. The children can then color in the sections with various colors of their crayons. This activity helps children develop motor skills necessary for writing. Some children will want to draw the outlines themselves. The "windows," when mounted on black paper, make an attractive picture.

# Jigsaw Puzzles

## Materials

- newspaper pictures (two of each picture)
- cover stock or cardboard
- felt marker
- blunt-edge scissors
- paste
- large envelopes

Collect two of the same full-page pictures usually found on the cover or inside the magazine section of the Sunday paper. Mount the pictures on cover stock or cardboard. Show the children how to use a felt marker to draw random lines across the face of one of the pictures to create a jigsaw puzzle. Cut the picture apart along the black lines that have been drawn. Four to six pieces are enough for a young child. Keep the second picture whole and use as a model to help children complete the picture puzzle. Put identifying marks on the reverse side of the puzzle pieces. These marks will help keep the pieces of the puzzle together after you have cut it apart. It will also avoid a mix-up if you plan to do this activity with other pictures as well. Children can put the puzzles together as a group or individually. Store the puzzles in large envelopes.

# Building Basic Concepts Through Photographs

## Materials

- newspaper pictures and advertisement supplements
- blunt-edge scissors
- construction paper
- paste
- *Dots, Spots, Speckles and Stripes* by Tana Hoban

**P**icture books illustrated with photographs can help children build basic concepts. For example, read *Dots, Spots, Speckles and Stripes* by Tana Hoban (published by Greenwillow books) to the youngsters. Then help children locate and cut out pictures in the newspaper that show dots, spots, speckles, and stripes. Advertisements are a good source. Find additional basic concept books by Tana Hoban and other photojournalists to serve as a stimulus for similar searches. Make a bulletin-board display or book of the children's findings, including the names of the children who participated in the project.

# Special Occasion Plates or Posters

## Materials

- newspaper
- paste
- paper plates, paper trays, or posters
- laminating material or clear pressure-sensitive plastic film
- blunt-edge scissors

**H**ighlight special occasions in the children's lives, such as birthdays and holidays. Ask children to paste newspaper clippings of the "hottest" news of their day on a large paper plate, paper tray, or poster. Be sure to include the newspaper's dateline.

Laminate the completed collages. As an alternative, cover the collages with clear pressure-sensitive film. These collages become treasured mementos of a special day.

# MAKING BARE BOOKS AND SHAPE BOOKS

# Bare Books

## Materials

- newspaper
- legal-size blank paper (8 ½" x 14")
- crayons
- manila folders or large envelopes
- stapler and staples
- blunt-edge scissors
- paste

Children enjoy making their own books. Bare books are a fine place to paste pictures cut from the newspaper. Children can write captions for the pictures they select as well. If the books they've made are kept throughout the year, you will have a fine record of the children's progress and they will have a nice remembrance of their work.

Bare books can be made by stapling several sheets of blank paper together. Legal-size paper (8 ½" x 14") makes a nice size book when folded in half to 8 ½" x 7". Be sure the children print their names on the covers of their books. Provide a model for children to follow that shows how to spell and write their names.

Each child should have a manila folder or envelope to store the books-in-progress. Children can then work on their individual books for several days until they are completed.

# Making a Shape Book

## Materials

- newspaper
- cover stock or oaktag
- construction paper (various colors)
- stapler or hole punch
- loose-leaf rings

- paste
- crayons
- yarn, string, or paper fasteners
- blunt-edge scissors

Shape books are fun for the children. Decide what category you are going to feature and provide a model. A book shaped like a house is a good starting point.

Use cover stock or oaktag for the front and back covers. Colored construction paper can be cut to the same shape for inside pages.

For a house book, children cut out newspaper pictures of furniture for the various rooms: kitchen, living room, bedroom, bathroom, etc. They then paste the pictures on the different pages. The name of each room can be written at the top or bottom of the page.

Books can be fastened by stapling or by punching holes in the side and tying with yarn or string. Paper fasteners or loose-leaf rings are another way of keeping the pages of the book together.

# Food Shape Books

## Materials

- food pages of the newspaper
- cover stock
- blunt-edge scissors
- paste
- crayons
- sheets of paper
- stapler and staples or paper fasteners

**F**ood shape books can help children learn about categories. The food pages in the newspaper, and the supplementary sections of food-page advertisements from various markets, will be useful for this project.

Food category books might include "My Fruit Book," "My Vegetable Book," and "My Cookie Book." A "Cereal Book" in the shape of a box of cereal, for example, could have newspaper pictures and the names of several different cereals. These pictures and names could then be categorized as to whether they are hot cereals or cold.

# A Book for Clothes

## Materials

- newspaper pictures of clothes
- paste
- crayons
- blunt-edge scissors
- sheets of paper
- stapler and staples or paper fasteners
- cover stock

The cover of this shape book could be a closet door with a doorknob. For the inside pages, the children can paste newspaper pictures of clothes. Smaller objects may be placed two on a page. The youngsters should label the pictures or have an adult label the pictures for them, if necessary.

# A Pairs Book

## Materials

- newspaper pictures of pairs
- blunt-edge scissors
- paste
- bare books

**H**ave children look through the newspaper and find pictures of pairs of things. They can then paste these pairs in their bare books. Examples could be pictures of pairs of shoes, gloves, earmuffs, slippers, sneakers, mittens, socks, and stockings.

A discussion could be generated about scissors and glasses. Why are they called a pair of scissors and a pair of glasses? These could also be included in the pairs books.

# LETTERS AND WORDS

# Cutting Out Letters and Words

## Materials

- newspaper
- paste
- blunt-edge scissors
- large envelopes
- felt marker
- oaktag or cover stock cut into 3" x 8 ½" strips

Newspaper headlines and some advertisements provide large letters which can be cut up and rearranged to make different words and sentences. In preparation for this activity, together with the children, cut out a quantity of letters so that you have a good supply available. File the letters in individual large envelopes. Each letter should be clearly written with a felt marker, on the outside of the envelopes, so the letters can be appropriately stored.

As a starting activity, children can make name cards. Have the children find the letters for their own names and the names of other members of their family. Have the children paste the letters on 3" x 8½" strips of oaktag or cover stock. Show children a model card as an appropriate guide.

# Alphabet Line

## Materials

- letters cut from the newspaper
- long sheets of blank paper
- masking tape
- paste

Take a long sheet of blank paper and place it in a horizontal position. Tape it to the wall or chalkboard with masking tape. Help children place and paste letters that have been cut from the newspaper in alphabetical order on the paper. Start with capital letters and subsequently repeat the alphabet line with both uppercase and lowercase letters. Emphasize the alphabetical sequence by singing the alphabet song with the children.

# Alphabet Word Line

## Materials

- words cut from the newspaper
- long sheet of blank paper
- masking tape
- paste

Using the same format as used with the alphabet line, help children make a word line in alphabetical sequence. As a variation, place the word line in a vertical or diagonal position. Use words that are cut from the newspaper. The advertisements usually have words in large typeface.

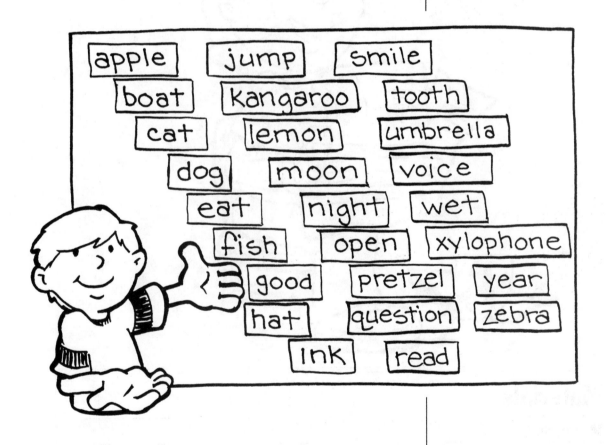

# Making a Letter-of-the-Alphabet Page

## Materials

- newspaper
- blunt-edge scissors
- paste
- drawing paper or blank paper
- crayons

**H**ave children cut out all the words they find in the newspaper beginning with a letter of their choice. It could be the first letter of their first or last names. Ask the children to paste the words on a piece of drawing paper and then paste a newspaper frame around the words. Display the letter pictures.

# Alphabet Books

## Materials

- newspaper
- construction paper (various colors)
- yarn
- blunt-edge scissors
- paste
- stapler or paper punch

**F**old various colored sheets of construction paper in half to make an alphabet book. Help the children write a letter of the alphabet at the top of each page. Use yarn to hold the book together or staple the pages together on one side.

Then have the children cut out words from the newspaper beginning with the letter of the alphabet at the top of each page and then paste the words on the appropriate pages. Demonstrate how to do this with model pages.

This can be an ongoing activity over a long period of time. When children are finished, they will have a great alphabet book!

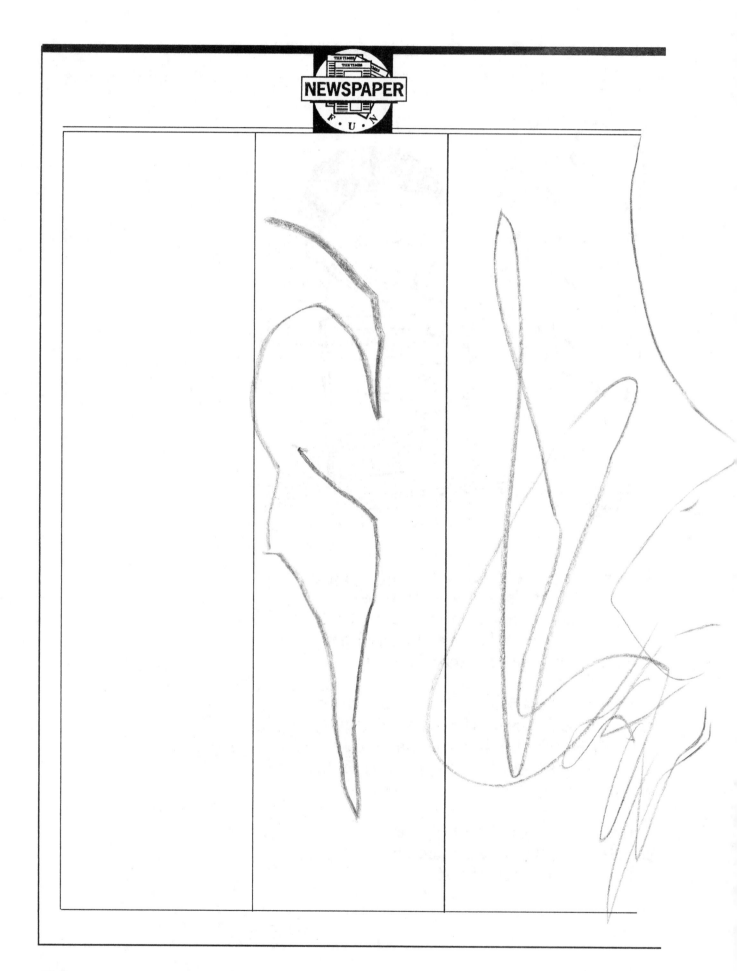

# WORD SKILLS

# Compound Words

## Materials

- newspaper
- blunt-edge scissors
- paste
- crayons or pencils
- bare books

Explain to the children that compound words are words that can be separated into two words that stand on their own. Have children search the newspaper for compound words. The children cut and paste the compound words in their bare books and rewrite each word by splitting it at the appropriate place.

# Double Consonants

## Materials

- newspaper
- blunt-edge scissors
- bare books
- paste
- crayons or pencils

**F**ind words in the newspaper that have double consonant letters in them. A good source is the sports page. Have the children cut out the double consonant words and paste them in a bare book. Explain to the children that if they have to separate a double consonant word when writing it, they should split the word between the two consonants that are alike. After pasting the double consonant words in their bare books, the words can be rewritten by the children showing how they can be divided.

# Words That Have a Final *y* That Sounds Like Long *e*

## Materials

- newspaper
- sheet of paper
- paste
- blunt-edge scissors

# Words That Have a Final *y* That Sounds Like Long *e*

**H**ave the children cut out words from the newspaper that have a final *y* that sounds like long *e*. Then have them paste these words on a sheet of paper to make a list. At the end of a designated period of time, see which child has the longest list. Children can work together in pairs, if they so desire.

# Syllabication

## Materials

- newspaper
- blunt-edge scissors
- paste
- sheets of paper

- chart paper
- chalk or felt marker
- crayons

**E**xplain to the children how words can be broken into parts called *syllables*. Start by having children count the syllables in their names. They can clap out the syllables as they say their names out loud. Tina would have 2 claps, Sylvia 3 claps, Elizabeth 4 claps, Alexandria 5 claps, Sam 1 clap, and so on.

With the children, locate multisyllable words in the newspaper. List them in categories on a wall chart or on the chalkboard as shown.

one syllable
bat

two syllables
honey

three syllables
newspapers

four syllables
categories

An individual syllable chart can be made by folding an 8 ½" x 11" sheet of paper held horizontally into four columns labeled 1, 2, 3, and 4. Ask the children to find more multisyllable words in the newspaper. Have them cut out and paste these words onto their syllable sheets in the appropriate columns.

# Word Families

## Materials

- ■ newspaper
- ■ blunt-edge scissors
- ■ bare books
- ■ paste
- ■ crayons

**T**eaching word families is an easy way of helping children with word identification. Ask children to cut out letters from the newspaper to make a book. Use a separate page for each word family. List the words of each family in alphabetical order. Concentrate on one word family at a time. When children know one family, move on to another. Include short vowel word families for a, e, i, o, and u.

NEWSPAPER
F · U · N

# SENTENCES

# Using a Large Wall Pocket Chart

## Materials

- newspaper
- pocket chart
- oaktag strip roll
- marker
- masking tape

Select an interesting picture from the newspaper and have the children discuss the picture with you. Then, with the children, make up three or four sentences about this newspaper picture. Write the sentences on oaktag strip roll. Place the strips in the pockets of a large wall pocket chart. If a wall chart is not available, attach the strips to the chalkboard with masking tape.

Read the sentences together with the children. If the sequence suggested by the children is not appropriate, discuss the sequence with them and rearrange the strips in a more logical order. Reread the sentences with the group.

# Making an Individual Pocket Chart

## Materials

- ■ newspaper letters and words
- ■ shoebox lids
- ■ pre-cut cardboard strips
- ■ paste
- ■ blunt-edge scissors

Vocabulary words should not be taught in isolation. Using sentence strips in a pocket chart can help avoid this. Children get the rhythm, flow, and meaning of language if they read new words in a meaningful context. Children can start constructing simple sentences from newspaper words. The use of the pocket chart also reinforces that in the English language we read from left to right.

To make an individual pocket chart, use the cover of a shoebox. On the inside lid, have the children paste cardboard strips across from side to side. Paste only the bottom part of the strip, so that the top remains open to form the pocket. Each child should have his or her own individual chart. Children can identify their own charts by cutting the letters for their names out of the newspaper and pasting the letters on top of the box lids.

# READING AND WRITING

# Figurative Language

## Materials

- ◼ newspaper
- ◼ *Amelia Bedelia* by Peggy Parish
- ◼ *The King Who Rained* by Fred Gwynne
- ◼ *A Chocolate Moose for Dinner* by Fred Gwynne

**R**ead books to the class, such as the *Amelia Bedelia* stories by Peggy Parish (published by HarperCollins and Greenwillow Books) and *The King Who Rained* and *A Chocolate Moose for Dinner* by Fred Gwynne (published by Simon & Schuster) to develop an awareness of figurative language. Help the children find examples in the newspaper of figurative language. Headlines are particularly good for this, as are story captions. Encourage the children to select one of the newspaper examples and illustrate it. Be sure to have them include the figurative expression.

# Building Vocabulary Through Newspaper Photographs

## Materials

- newspaper
- blunt-edge scissors
- drawing or construction paper
- crayons

- paste
- *On Monday When It Rained* by
  Cherryl Kachenmeister

**R**ead *On Monday When It Rained* by Cherryl Kachenmeister (published by Houghton Mifflin) to the children. As a follow-up activity, have the youngsters locate pictures from the newspaper reflecting people's feelings. Ask the children to cut the pictures out of the newspaper and paste them on drawing or construction paper.

Help the children label the pictures with an appropriate word that reflects the facial expression. The sports pages are a good source.

# The Five W's

## Materials

- ■ newspaper articles
- ■ various color markers
- ■ pencils
- ■ paper

Select a brief article from the newspaper and read it together with the children. It would be helpful if multiple copies of the newspaper are available. Discuss the contents of the article and point out how the headline highlights the main idea. Explain that a well-written article should contain the five w's: who, what, when, where, and why.

Reread the story with the group and circle with different color markers the who, what, when, where, and why. Repeat this with different examples over a period of time using the same procedure.

Encourage the children to write brief articles for their own class or family mini-newspaper. Have children write headlines for their stories and credit them with a by-line. Photocopy the mini-newspaper to distribute to family and friends.

# GOING MARKETING WITH THE NEWSPAPER

# Grocery Shopping

## Materials

- newspaper food advertisements
- large brown paper bags
- paste
- blunt-edge scissors

**F**or a variation from making books, children can use large brown paper bags from the grocery store to mount pictures of food cut from the newspaper. Suggest that children paste the pictures on the bag in the sequence that they would use if they were shopping in a store. For example, ice cream would be the last picture pasted to the bag. Ice cream would melt if it were put in the cart before children did the rest of their marketing.

# Categorizing Pictures

## Materials

- ■ newspaper food advertisements
- ■ blunt-edge scissors
- ■ paste
- ■ chart paper or posterboard
- ■ felt marker

**H**ave the children cut out food pictures from the newspaper and arrange them in categories. The pictures can be pasted by category on a large chart.

# How Much Does It Cost?

## Materials

- ■ newspaper food advertisements with prices
- ■ chalk
- ■ chalkboard

**D**istribute the food section of the newspaper that has the prices of groceries. Discuss with the children what foods they like to eat for breakfast. List the foods on the chalkboard. Then have the children find the prices of these items in the newspaper advertisements. Write the prices next to the items on the board as the children dictate them to you.

# What Costs More Than a Dollar?

## Materials

- ■ newspaper food advertisements with prices
- ■ chart paper or posterboard
- ■ felt marker
- ■ masking tape

**L**ook at food advertisements in the newspaper with the children. Discuss with them the cost of various foods. Then set up four columns on a chart. The columns could be as follows:

| Food Item | Quantity | Price under $1.00 | Price over $1.00 |
|-----------|----------|-------------------|------------------|
| milk | quart | $.78 | |
| eggs | 1 dozen | | $1.44 |

   Prices will vary from store to store. Ask the children to tell you which items are under or over a dollar. Record the prices on the chart.

# Let's Play Store

## Materials

- ■ newspaper with food pictures
- ■ blunt-edge scissors
- ■ cover stock
- ■ paste

Children can have fun with imaginative play in setting up a little store. They can stock their store with large pictures of fruits, vegetables, and household supplies from the newspaper. After cutting out pictures with a blunt-edge scissors, children can paste the pictures onto cover stock. Pasting the pictures onto two pieces of cover stock (cut to shape), one on top of the other, will give a rigidity that withstands handling.

# USING CARTOONS AND COMICS TO TEACH VOCABULARY AND COMPREHENSION

# Developing Verbal Skills

## Materials

- ■ newspaper with wordless comic strips
- ■ oaktag or cover stock
- ■ paste
- ■ laminating material or clear pressure-sensitive plastic film

**W**ith the children, locate the comics section in the
newspaper by using the index. Cut out the wordless
comic strips and mount them as a whole on oaktag
or cover stock. Discuss the comic strips with the
children to develop their verbal skills and
comprehension of these picture stories. If possible,
laminate the pictures or cover them with clear
plastic to withstand usage.

# Making a Comics Collection

## Materials

- ■ newspaper cartoons or comics
- ■ paste
- ■ bare books
- ■ blunt-edge scissors

**H**ave the children cut out and paste their favorite cartoons or comics in one of their bare books. If there is a special strip with a continuing story, the children may want to put these comics in one book. Non-related comics and cartoons could be mounted in another. This is an appealing on-going activity.

# Sequence

## Materials

- ■ newspaper cartoons or comics
- ■ paste
- ■ bare books
- ■ oaktag
- ■ laminating material or clear pressure-sensitive plastic film

**D**iscuss with the children that most comic strips consist of a series of frames that are connected to tell a story. Then cut up a comic strip into sections and mount each section on oaktag. Children can then reconstruct the story by putting the frames in the proper sequence. Mount the same strip as a whole on another piece of oaktag. Children can then check to see that they have put the story together properly.

You can protect the oaktag strips by covering them with clear pressure-sensitive film.

# Who Said What?

## Materials

- newspaper cartoons
- blunt-edge scissors
- paste
- cover stock or cardboard

Cut cartoons from the newspaper and paste them on cover stock or cardboard. Remove the words of the cartoons and mount them separately. Have the children match the words to the appropriate pictures. This activity is particularly good for developing comprehension skills.

A duplicate set of cards should be made up with the cartoons intact. This can serve as a self-checking activity when the children are working on their own.

# Contractions

## Materials

- ■ newspaper comics
- ■ crayons or felt markers
- ■ chart tablet
- ■ chalk
- ■ chalkboard

**E**xplain to the children that sometimes two words are put together to make one word. Give examples, such as *can't* for *cannot, won't* for *will not, we're* for *we are,* etc. Then read the comics together and circle words that are contractions. These contractions can then be listed on the chalkboard or chart tablet for the children to reread later.

# Recognizing Cartoon and Comic Strip Characters

## Materials

- newspaper advertisements
- blunt-edge scissors
- paste
- construction paper
- crayons
- sheets of paper
- stapler

**M**any cartoon and comic strip characters appear in the newspaper in advertisements for various products. To locate familiar characters, have children look through the newspaper, including the business section. Ask children to cut out pictures of cartoon characters they recognize and mount them on construction paper. They can then label them as well. When a sufficient number of characters have been collected, children can collate them into a class book. List the names of the children who participated in the project on the cover.

# FUN WITH NUMBERS

# Numbers

## Materials

- ■ newspaper
- ■ blunt-edge scissors
- ■ paste
- ■ oaktag or cardboard
- ■ paper

Have children cut out numbers from the newspaper and put them in a sequence. The children can then paste the numbers in various sequences on paper, oaktag, or cardboard.

# Television Time

## Materials

- newspaper
- chart paper
- felt marker

**Television Chart**

| # | SHOW | TIME | ST |
|---|------|------|-----|
| 1 | COSBY | | |
| 2 | Full House | | |
| 3 | Home Video | | |
| 4 | Double Dare | | |
| 5 | Darkwing Duck | | |
| 6 | Doug | | |
| 7 | Brady Bunch | | |
| 8 | Carmen San Diego | | |
| 9 | Simpsons | | |
| 10 | Wheel of Fortune | | |

**W**ith the children, locate the television news section in the newspaper by using the index. Discuss which programs the children enjoy watching. Have children select the time and station of one program they enjoy. Record their favorites on a chart.

# Read-Together Time

## Materials

- newspaper
- blunt-edge scissors
- paste
- paper plate
- paper
- paper fastener

Cut out numbers 1 to 12 from the newspaper and paste them on a paper plate in the proper space to make a clock face. Then fasten two strips of paper to the center of the plate with a paper fastener to make clock hands. Have the children set the hands to their family or class read-together time.

# Opinion Polls

## Materials

- newspaper
- graph paper
- crayon or pencil
- ruler

Study different graphs in the newspaper with the children. For the young child, a bar graph is the easiest to understand. The children can conduct a survey and develop their own bar graphs. One topic might be to find out people's favorite ice-cream flavors. Another suggestion is to ask children to select their favorite comic strips. Together, develop a bar graph on graph paper to record the results of the survey.

# Number Book

## Materials

- newspaper pictures
- blunt-edge scissors
- paste
- crayons
- bare books

**A** number book can be made from a bare book. Have children paste a picture cut from the newspaper of one object on page one, two objects on page two, and so on. Encourage children to write the numeral and the number name on the appropriate page. Have children write their names on the cover of the book as well.

# HOW'S THE WEATHER?

# Weather Maps

## Materials

- ■ newspaper
- ■ pencil
- ■ paper
- ■ crayons

**H**ave the children locate the weather map in the newspaper by looking up the page in the index. It would be helpful if there were several copies of the newspaper available. Children could work in pairs. Develop the children's map skills by locating cities in the north, south, east, and west, as well as the central states. Find the cities with the greatest variation in temperature: hottest, coldest, etc. Have the children record the information on a sheet of paper.

# My Weather Chart

## Materials

- newspaper
- blunt-edge scissors
- paste
- oaktag
- yarn
- bead

**F**ind the weather symbols on the weather page of the newspaper or on the masthead of the first page. Cut the symbols out and paste them on a piece of oaktag. String a piece of yarn with a bead on it under the pictures. Have the children move the bead to the appropriate weather each day.

# Design Their Own Weather Pictures

## Materials

- newspaper
- paper
- crayons

**V**iew weather symbols in the newspaper with the children. If a variety of newspapers is brought into class, children can compare the weather symbols of the different papers. Then have the children draw their own pictures for different kinds of weather. This can be done by folding a sheet of paper into four sections. Label the sections "sunny," "rainy," "windy," and "snowy." Have the youngsters fill in the boxes with their own symbols of the weather patterns.

# Highlighting a Windy Day

## Materials

- newspaper
- blunt-edge scissors
- drawing paper
- crayons
- paste

**A** fun activity for children is to cut out shapes of clothes from the newspaper and then hang them on a clothesline.  On a sheet of drawing paper, have the children draw a clothesline held up by two posts.  Then have them "hang" the newspaper clothes they have cut out by pasting them on the line.

This can lead to a science talk about how water from wet clothes will evaporate into the air.

# SUGGESTIONS AND CONCLUSION

# Suggestions

Save the fun pages and any children's sections from the newspaper in a special file for rainy-day activities. You and the children will both be glad you did.

Have a little box or basket for the supplies you and the children will need to implement the suggestions in this book. A shopping bag is useful for holding extra newspapers. Put the youngsters' names on their boxes and bags. This way, they will know which is their very own supply kit, always ready and available for them to use.

Supplies you will find helpful include:

- newspapers, cartoons, and comic strips
- blunt-edge scissors
- paste or paste stick
- pencils and thick crayons
- felt markers of various colors
- drawing paper
- construction paper of various colors
- paper plates
- brown paper grocery bags
- oaktag or cardboard
- plain envelopes
- hole puncher
- clips and paper fasteners
- stapler and staples
- yarn and string
- pressure-sensitive tape
- pressure-sensitive clear film
- graph paper
- oaktag strip roll
- ruler
- masking tape
- loose-leaf rings

Save all the loose-page activities that are not already assembled in books and collate them to make a class or home big book. Label this "The Big Book of Newspaper Activities." Have the children print their names on the cover, or have them cut their names out from newspaper letters and paste them to the cover. The book can be held together with loose-leaf rings. Children will enjoy reading and rereading what they have created in their own big book, and so will you!

REMEMBER: YOUNG CHILDREN'S ACTIVITIES SHOULD ALWAYS BE SUPERVISED!

# Conclusion

It is important to develop an awareness in the children and their parents to watch for things in the newspaper that reinforce the activities in *Newspaper Fun: Activities for Young Children.* By being on the alert, children, parents, and teachers really begin to appreciate the wealth of information that can be obtained each day from a very current and available resource—the newspaper! ■

Name _____

A B C D E F G H I J K L M N O P Q R S T U V W X Y Z

a b c d e f g h i j k l m n o p q r s t u v w x y z

## Writing Letters

A _____

a _____

B _____

b _____

Letter Knowledge

A | **Writing Letters** | a b c d e f g h i j

B
C
D
E
F
G
H
I
J
K
L
M
N
O
P

k
l
m
n
o
p
q
r
s
t
u
v
w
x

C

c

D

d

E

e

Q R S T U V W X Y Z z y

Name

A B C D E F G H I J K L M N O P Q R S T U V W X Y Z

a b c d e f g h i j k l m n o p q r s t u v w x y z

Writing Letters

F

f

G

g

H

h

Letter Knowledge

Name

**Writing Letters** a b c d e f g h i j

A B C D E F G H I J K L M N O

k l m n o p q r s t u v w x y

I

i

J

j

K

k

P Q R S T U V W X Y Z z y

Copyright © 1995 Open Court Publishing Company

Writing Letters   a b c d e f g h i j

A B C D E F G H I J K L M N O

P Q R S T U V W X Y Z

k l m n o p q r s t u v w x z y

L

I

M

m

N

n

Writing Letters a b c d e f g h i j

O

o

P

p

Q

q

a b c d e f g h i j k l m n o p q r s t u v w x y

A B C D E F G H I J K L M N O P Q R S T U V W X Y Z z

Name

Writing Letters

a b c d e f g h i j k l m n o p q r s t u v w x y z

A B C D E F G H I J K L M N O P Q R S T U V W X Y Z

R

r

S

s

I

t

Letter Knowledge

R/WC 7

Writing Letters

A B C D E F G H I J K L M N O P

a b c d e f g h i j k l m n o p q r s t u v w x y

U

u

V

v

W

w

Q R S T U V W X Y Z z

Writing Letters a b c d e f g h i j

X

x

Y

y

Z

Z

*Phonics*

a ★   b   c   d   e   f   g   h   i   j   k   l   m

n   o   p   q   r   s   t   u   v   w   x   y   z

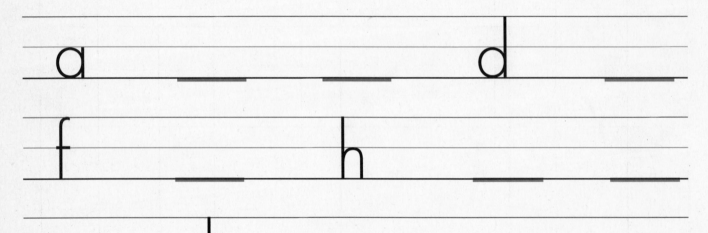

a _ _ _ d _ _ _

f _ _ h _ _ _

_ l m _ _ o

p _ _ _ s t

u _ _ _ x _ z

B

C

A ★

D

E

F

G

H

I

V

W

J

U

X

K

T

Y

M

N

O

P

Q

L

R

S

Z

B    C    E

G    I    J

K    N

Q    R

V    W    Y

## Sounds and Spellings

m

m

M

## Listening for Consonants

# Name

## Listening for Consonants

_____ _____

_____ _____

_____ _____

_____ _____

_____ _____

_____ _____

_____ _____

_____ _____

Consonant Sounds and Spellings

**Lesson 12**

## Sounds and Spellings

a

a

A

I am

I am in a

### Reading

I am on the

I am in the

I am a ____.

I am in the

I am on the

I am a ____.

I am on the

I am in the

I am a ____.

Name

Sounds and Spellings

t

t

T

Writing Words and Sentences

at _____

mat _____

I am at

_____

_____

Consonant Sounds and Spellings

## Listening for Consonants

_____ _____

_____ _____

_____ _____

_____ _____

_____ _____

_____ _____

_____ _____

_____ _____

_____ _____

_____ _____

_____ _____

_____ _____

_____ _____

_____ _____

_____ _____

_____ _____

_____ _____

_____ _____

_____ _____

_____ _____

_____ _____

_____ _____

_____ _____

_____ _____

Consonant Sounds and Spellings

## Sounds and Spellings

h_

h

H

## Completing Sentences

A tam is a _____.

Matt has a _____.

# Name

## Listening for Consonants

_____
_____

_____
_____

_____
_____

_____
_____
_____

_____
_____
_____

_____
_____

_____
_____
_____

_____
_____

_____
_____

Consonant Sounds and Spellings

## Sounds and Spellings

p

p

P

## Writing Words and Sentences

pat

tap

Pam has a map.

### Reading and Writing

Pat has a hat.

Pam is at the map.

_____

_____

_____

I tap my hat.

Pat is on a mat.

_____

_____

_____

I tap the can.

Pat has a hat.

_____

_____

_____

*Phonics*

## Sounds and Spellings

n

n

N

## Writing Words and Sentences

nap _____

man _____

Nan has a nap.

Completing Sentences

 I nap on a _____.

| ham |
| mat |

 The man has a _____.

| tap |
| tam |

 Pam has a _____.

| hat |
| nap |

 Pat has a _____.

| pan |
| map |

 The ant is on the _____.

| hat |
| ham |

 Nat has a _____.

| nap |
| pan |

Blending

*Phonics*

# Name

## Sounds and Spellings

c

c

C

## Writing Words and Sentences

cat

cap

Can the cat tap on the can?

Consonant Sounds and Spellings

*Phonics*

Writing Words

_____
_____
_____

_____
_____
_____

Nan can pat the _____.

Pam has a _____.

Name

Sounds and Spellings

d

d

D

Writing Words and Sentences

dad            mad

Dad had a hat.

Consonant Sounds and Spellings

Copyright © 1995 Open Court Publishing Company

Writing Words and Sentences

hat

hand

pan

_____

cap

map

Dad

_____

_____

Dad has a cap.
Dan can nap.
The cat can nap.

_____

_____

_____

## Sounds and Spellings

s

s _____

S _____

## Writing Words and Sentences

sat _____     sand _____

Sam is sad.

_____

_____

_____

## Writing Words

## Drawing

# The hats are on the cats.

## Sounds and Spellings

i

i

I

## Writing Words and Sentences

him

tips

Tim sits in the sand.

Vowel Sounds and Spelling

*Phonics*

# Name

## Writing and Reading

_____
_____
_____

_____
_____
_____

_____
_____
_____

_____
_____
_____

pin    map    stamp    mints    picnic    cap

Completing Sentences

Sid _____ a handstand.

Nan sat on the _____.

Sam has a _____.

Decoding

Sounds and Spellings

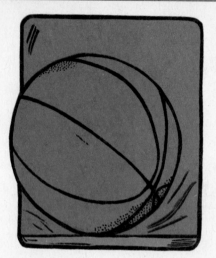

b

b

B

Writing Words and Sentences

bib

bands

A bat was a bit sad.

**Reading and Writing**

bat

bats

bit

_____

_____

pin

pit

pan

_____

_____

Sid sat in the sand.

Nan and Min had
a picnic.

_____

_____

_____

_____

Blending/Decoding

Name

Sounds and Spellings

r

r

R

Writing Words and Sentences

rip                    trip

A rat bit the cat and ran.

Copyright © 1995 Open Court Publishing Company

Name

## Reading and Writing

Brad ran on the ramp.

The rabbit is in the crib.

Min ran at camp.

Tim is on a trip.

Sid stands in the sand.

Sid can stand on his hands.

*Phonics*

Blending

## Sounds and Spellings

f

f

F

## Writing Words and Sentences

fan          fat

# Can the fat cat fit in the hat?

*Phonics*

## Writing and Reading

_____
_____
_____

_____
_____
_____

_____
_____
_____

_____
_____
_____

Blending

## Sounds and Spellings

g

g

G

## Writing Words and Sentences

gas                    grab

The pig is big.

## Writing Words

pig

gas

grin

tag

dig

big

## Listening for Vowels

_i_                    _a_

_____        _____

_____        _____

_____        _____

_____        _____

_____        _____

_____        _____

_____        _____

Vowel Sounds and Spellings

## Writing Words

_____

_____

_____

_____

_____

_____

_____

_____

_____

| cabin |
| hatpin |
| rabbit |

## Completing Sentences

Dad _____ the cat.

fins
fans

The pig can _____ in the bag.

fat
fit

Blending

*Phonics*

# Name

**Lesson 27**

## Sounds and Spellings

# The dog can stop the top.

Vowel Sounds and Spellings

44 R/WC

*Phonics*

## Reading and Writing

Dad can spin a _____.

| tip |
| top |
| tap |

Pam and Sam _____ the pig.

| pit |
| pot |
| pat |

## Dictation and Spelling

_____     _____

_____     _____

_____     _____

_____     _____

_____     _____

_____     _____

*Phonics*

Decoding/Spelling

## Sounds and Spellings

 x

## Writing Words and Sentences

fox _____

mix _____

The ax is in the box.

Copyright © 1995 Open Court Publishing Company

*Phonics*

# Name

## Listening for Vowels

_i_          _a_          _o_

_____   _____   _____

_____   _____   _____

_____   _____   _____

_____   _____   _____

_____   _____   _____

_____   _____   _____

_____   _____   _____

Vowel Sounds and Spellings

Lesson 29

**Reading and Writing**

The fox sat on the mat.

The fox has six ants.

An ax is in the box.

Max has an ax.

The cat was in the mix.

The cat sits in the box.

Dad can fix the map.

Dan taps the mix.

## Writing Words

frog

pan

box

_____   _____   _____

_____   _____   _____

## Dictation and Spelling

_____   _____

_____   _____

_____   _____

_____   _____

_____   _____

_____

_____

Decoding/Spelling

Sounds and Spellings

ar

Writing Words and Sentences

 _____

 _____

 _____

 _____

# The car is in the barn.

_____

_____

_____

## Writing Words

farm

star

ram

barn

man

rabbit

frog

ax

_____   _____   _____

_____   _____   _____

_____   _____   _____

_____   _____   _____

_____   _____   _____

_____   _____   _____

_____   _____   _____

## Sounds and Spellings

c

ck

## Writing Words

s    st    p    r    sn    d    tr

_ack          _ick          _ock

## Reading and Writing Sentences

Rick has socks in the sack.
She picks a stick from the stack.

_____

_____

_____

_____

## Dictation and Spelling

_____     _____

_____     _____

_____     _____

_____     _____

_____

_____

## Sounds and Spellings

u

u

U

## Writing Words and Sentences

bug          drum

The duck is stuck in the mud.

*Phonics*

Name _____

Reading and Writing Sentences

She scrubs the pup's rug.
She hugs the pup.

_____

_____

Bud dug in the sun.
The bug runs up the pump.

_____

_____

It is fun to jump in the tub.
She drops her duck in the tub.

_____

_____

_____

_____

Vowel Sounds and Spellings

*Phonics*

Sounds and Spellings

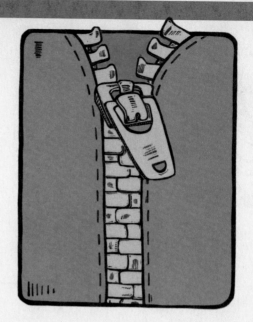

z

z

Z

Writing Words and Sentences

zip          buzz

The bug ran in a zigzag.

Consonant Sounds and Spellings

*Phonics*

## Word Study

Pam   pup   robin   rat

## Dictation and Spelling

Decoding/Spelling

Completing Sentences

off    dress    buzz    add    grass    fizz
puff    Ann    sniff    huff    pass

1. Did you rip the _____ _____?

2. Max sat in the _____.

3. Does the bug _____?

4. The top is _____ the box.

5. The dog will _____ the bug.

6. Dan said, "_____ it to me!"

7. I can _____ six and six.

8. Hand the cup _____ to _____ .

9. Do you _____ and _____ as you run?

Name

Sounds and Spellings

l

I

L

Writing Words and Sentences

last ————    tickle ————

Bill slips in the puddle.

Consonant Sounds and Spellings

Copyright © 1995 Open Court Publishing Company

*Phonics*

## Reading and Writing Sentences

Lil fills the pickle jar.
Liz has lots of dolls.

## Dictation and Spelling

Sounds and Spellings

e

E

Writing Words and Sentences

hen         tent

neck       sled

The egg fell on the bed.

Vowel Sounds and Spellings

## Writing Words

_____

_____

_____

_____

_____

_____

_____

_____

_____

_____

_____

_____

_____

_____

_____

_____

# An insect has _____ legs.

_____

_____

_____

_____

_____

_____

_____

_____

_____

Completing Sentences

| instead | head | spread | fed | dead |

1. Ted _____ jam on his bread.

2. "The bug is _____," said Meg.

3. Greg _____ the red hen.

4. Peg will run _____ of Ben.

5. Can you fix the puppet's _____?

*Phonics*

# Name

## Writing Words

left    bed    instead    bread    nest

_____

_____

## Dictation and Spelling

**Lesson 38**

Sounds and Spellings

Y–

Y

Y

Writing Words and Sentences

yam

yes

yell

yet

The cat has yards of yarn.

Consonant Sounds and Spellings

*Phonics*

Name _____

Reading and Writing Sentences

1.  2.  3.

The dog yelps at the rabbit.
A rabbit nibbles plants in the yard.
The dog naps in the backyard.

_____

1. _____

_____

_____

2. _____

_____

_____

3. _____

_____

*Phonics*

Decoding

R/WC 67

Sounds and Spellings

W_

w

W

Writing Words and Sentences

wet                    wag

wiggle                 well

Will you get a wagon?

Consonant Sounds and Spellings

*Phonics*

Name

Sounds and Spellings

wh_

when          whiz

Dictation and Spelling

Decoding/Spelling

Sounds and Spellings

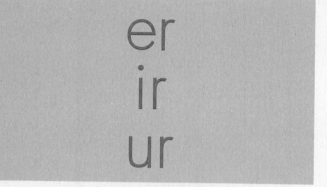

er
ir
ur

Writing Words and Sentences

her _____      bird _____

girl _____      sister _____

curl _____      turn _____

Bert had a hamburger for supper.

_____

_____

_____

Vowel Sounds and Spellings

*Phonics*

# Name

## Unscrambling Sentences

saw    girl    a
The    turtle.    little

nest.    bird    sits    on
purple    a    The

Word Study

| a e u | a i o | e i o |
|---|---|---|
| st__p | d__sh | t__p |
| d__st | p__nd | br__ck |
| st__nd | l__nd | b__st |

| a i o | e o u | i o u |
|---|---|---|
| w__sh | b__g | l__ck |
| y__m | dr__p | f__sh |
| fr__g | h__lp | t__b |

## Completing Sentences

better
butter

1. Sam had bread and _____ .

stepped
stopped

2. Mom _____ the car.

packed
pecked

3. Herb _____ his bag.

dig
dog

4. The girls _____ in the dirt.

## Dictation and Spelling

_____    _____

_____    _____

_____    _____

_____    _____

_____    _____

_____    _____

_____    _____

_____

Name

Sounds and Spellings

sh

Writing Words and Sentences

shop _____    shack _____

wish _____    crash _____

sharp _____    shiver _____

Sherman has six shells in a box.

## Writing Words

| dish | ship | shirt | fresh | shell | brush | fish |

_____

_____

_____

_____

_____

_____

Decoding

Sounds and Spellings

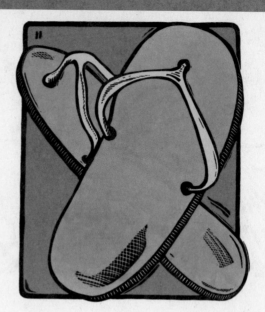

th

Writing Words and Sentences

thick _____          that _____

with _____          bath _____

thunder _____

This is a thin twig.

## Unscrambling Sentences

bird    feathers.    This    red    has

_____

_____

_____

_____

## Dictation and Spelling

_____    _____

_____    _____

_____    _____

_____    _____

_____    _____

_____    _____

Name _____

Sounds and Spellings

_____

ch

_____

Writing Words and Sentences

chin _____    church _____

chick _____    inch _____

chill _____    bunch _____

The children munch on chips.

_____

_____

_____

_____

## Writing Words

| check | chop | chimp | chicken |
|-------|------|-------|---------|
| ranch | bench | much | lunchbox |

_____

_____

_____

_____

_____

_____

_____

_____

_____

_____

_____

_____

_____

_____

_____

_____

_____

Decoding

Sounds and Spellings

ch

■tch

Writing Words and Sentences

fetch _____    switch _____

itch _____    stretch _____

Mitch catches the pitch.

_____

_____

Stitch a patch on the cap.

_____

_____

Name _____

## Writing Words

fetch  patches  crutches  catch  ditch  scratch

_____    _____    _____

_____    _____    _____

## Dictation and Spelling

_____    _____

_____    _____

_____    _____

_____    _____

_____    _____

_____    _____

_____    _____

_____    _____

Completing Sentences

| split | strip | splash | strap | splinter | scratches |

1. The frog jumped into the water with a _____.

2. Max has a _____ in his hand.

3. The carpenter cut a thin _____ of plastic.

4. The dog _____ its back.

Reading

# Patches and Dan

1. Dan pitches the stick.

2. Patches jumps to catch it.

3. The stick splashes in the pond.

4. Patches fetches the stick.

_____

_____

_____

_____

## Sounds and Spellings

c
ck
k

k

K

## Writing Words and Sentences

kick

bark

kitchen

silk

The kitten laps milk.

## Writing Words

park  kept  breakfast  mask  kick  kettle

_____  _____  _____

_____  _____  _____

_____  _____  _____

## Dictation and Spelling

_____  _____

_____  _____

_____  _____

_____  _____

_____  _____

_____

_____

_____

_____

## Sounds and Spellings

a

a_e

## Writing Words and Sentences

apron _____     ape _____

table _____     shape _____

cradle _____    skate _____

Dave made a mask with paper and tape.

_____

_____

_____

_____

Long Vowel Sounds and Spellings

*Phonics*

Completing Sentences

 1. Ted has a _____ on his head.

cap
cape

 2. Pat fixed his model _____ _____.

plan
plane

 3. A whale _____ swim.

can
cane

 4. Mark _____ muffins.

mad
made

 5. Kate has a _____ kitten.

fat
fate

*Phonics*

Sounds and Spellings

j

■dge

J

J

Writing Words and Sentences

job

juggle

judge

badge

Jake cut the tall hedge.

Copyright © 1995 Open Court Publishing Company

Name

## Reading and Writing Sentences

Jack's dad jogs across the bridge.

Jan jumps across the ditch.

_____

_____

_____

_____

## Dictation and Spelling

_____

_____

_____

_____

_____

_____

Decoding/Spelling

Name

Sounds and Spellings

j      ge

■dge    gi_

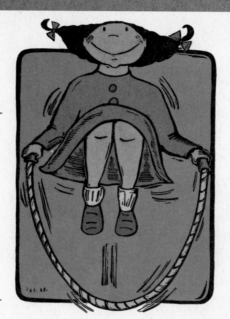

Writing Words and Sentences

gem _____    ginger _____

page _____    stage _____

The gerbil ran into the cage.

_____

_____

_____

_____

Consonant Sounds and Spellings

*Phonics*

Listening for Consonant Sounds

gag     judge     bridge     gave

gentle     bag     grip     badge

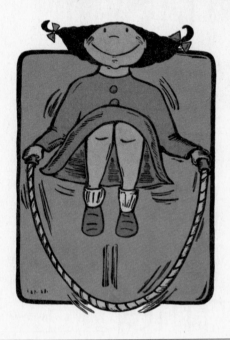 

_____

_____

_____

_____

_____

_____

_____

_____

_____

Decoding

## Sounds and Spellings

i

i_e

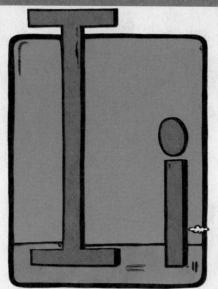

## Writing Words and Sentences

tiger _____        title _____

time _____        smile _____

Nine fish swim in the tide.

_____

Did you find the dime?

_____

Long Vowel Sounds and Spellings

*Phonics*

## Completing Sentences

1. I like to _____ a bike.

rid
ride

2. Did you _____ the page?

rip
ripe

3. Dad made a _____ dinner.

fin
fine

4. The man was gentle and _____.

kin
kind

## Dictation and Spelling

_____    _____

_____    _____

_____    _____

_____

_____

Decoding/Spelling

# Name

Sounds and Spellings

s

ce

ci__

Writing Words and Sentences

cent _____     circus _____

space _____     cider _____

Grace likes nice mice.

_____

_____

We danced in a circle.

_____

_____

### Listening for Consonant Sounds

face   cake   ice   candle   picnic
carrot   city   twice   circle

**Lesson 53**

Writing Opposites

| last | finished | soft | off |

1. The girl <u>started</u> the race. _____

2. Dad turned the lamp <u>on</u>. _____

3. Linda is <u>first</u> in line. _____

4. The bed is too <u>hard</u>. _____

Writing Synonyms

| little | ran | cut |

1. Dad will <u>trim</u> the hedge. _____

2. Is a gerbil <u>small</u>? _____

3. Kate <u>raced</u> up the hill. _____

## Name

### Writing Rhyming Words

line   mile   ice   cent

_____

_____

_____

### Dictation and Spelling

_____     _____

_____     _____

_____     _____

_____     _____

_____

_____

_____

_____

_____

Sounds and Spellings

Sounds and Spellings

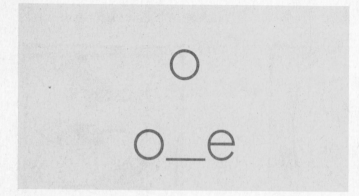

Writing Words and Sentences

no ———————    hold ———————

broke ———————    stone ———————

The dog hid the bone.

————————————————

————————————————

I told him to go home.

————————————————

————————————————

Listening for Words

○ April
○ open
○ oval

○ hop
○ hope
○ hold

○ block
○ bone
○ broke

○ acorn
○ apple
○ able

○ not
○ nice
○ notes

○ spoke
○ spot
○ spike

An octopus has _____ bones.

Sounds and Spellings

z

__s

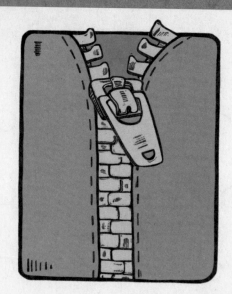

Writing Words

nose

eggs

chips    rose    this    has    mice    pins

## Writing Opposites

| open | no | white | close | yes | black |

_____        _____
_____        _____
_____        _____
_____        _____

## Dictation and Spelling

_____        _____
_____        _____
_____        _____
_____        _____

Decoding/Spelling

_Phonics_

Sounds and Spellings

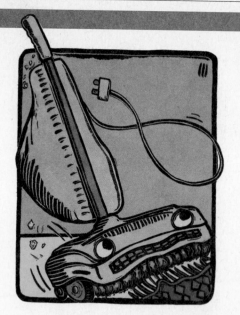

v

v

V

Writing Words and Sentences

vine _____          van _____

brave _____          five _____

Vince has seven valentines.

Completing Sentences

stove     drives     never

velvet     saves     vase

1. My mom _____ a van.

2. Jim _____ baseball cards.

3. Val has a _____ dress.

4. Lance put the pan on the

_____.

5. Put the buds in a _____.

# Name

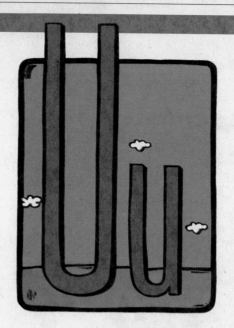

## Sounds and Spellings

u

u__e

## Writing Words and Sentences

use _____  bugle _____

cube _____  huge _____

The mule likes music.

_____

_____

Cute cats amuse Chuck.

_____

_____

Vowel Sounds and Spellings

*Phonics*

# Name

## Completing Sentences

The mule has a cute hat.

The mule licks an ice cube.

## Dictation and Spelling

**Lesson 58**

### Sounds and Spellings

e

e__e

### Writing Words and Sentences

she _____   these _____

even _____   equal _____

Pete sits here.

_____

Steve had a fever.

_____

Vowel Sounds and Spellings

*Phonics*

Reading and Writing

The giraffe has a huge neck.

Eve pets the giraffe.

_____

_____

_____

_____

_____

The man is skating.

The man is on the trapeze.

_____

_____

_____

_____

We sat on the fence.

Put a dime in the meter.

_____

_____

_____

*Phonics*

Decoding

cake    cape    cap

_____
_____
_____

help    here    hen

_____
_____

kitchen    kitten    kite

_____
_____
_____

rope    robber    rocket

_____
_____
_____

cute    cub    cube

_____
_____
_____

crane    crash    crate

_____
_____
_____

trapeze    tape    tap

_____
_____

Name

## Word Study

cap
cake
make

_____

_____

bike
kitten
kite

_____

_____

cube
cute
cut

_____

_____

nose
hose
rose

_____

_____

## Dictation and Spelling

_____ _____

_____ _____

_____ _____

_____ _____

_____ _____

_____

_____

_____

Decoding/Spelling

Sounds and Spellings

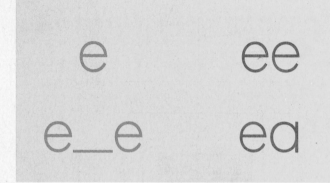

Writing Words and Sentences

eagle _____ meal _____

feel _____ sheep _____

Steve eats green beans.

_____

_____

The sneakers fit his feet.

_____

_____

Vowel Sounds and Spellings

*Phonics*

Writing Opposites

begin   awake   fake   far   real   remember
end   forget   freeze   near   melt   asleep

_____   _____

_____   _____

_____   _____

_____   _____

_____   _____

_____   _____

_____   _____

_____   _____

_____   _____

_____   _____

*Antonyms*

Name

Sounds and Spellings

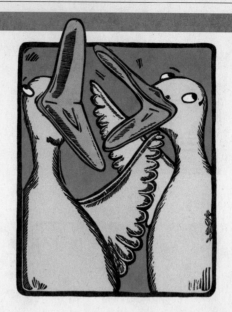

qu__

qu _____    Qu _____

Writing Words and Sentences

queen _____    quack _____

quiet _____    quit _____

The quilt is made of squares.

_____

_____

_____

_____

## Listening for Words

- ○ quit
- ○ quite
- ○ quiet

- ○ cake
- ○ quake
- ○ quack

- ○ liquid
- ○ licked
- ○ liked

## Dictation and Spelling

_____

_____

_____

_____

_____

_____

_____

_____

_____

_____

_____

_____

_____

_____

Decoding/Spelling

Word Study

| scare | squirrel | umpire | store |
| deer | more | scored | square |

1. A _____ gathers nuts

and hides them.

2. I'd like _____ ice cream.

3. Beth _____ three home runs.

4. Sam got his jacket at the _____.

5. A _____ has equal sides.

6. The _____ was at the baseball

game.

**Homophones**

1. I can _____ the music.

here   hear

2. Pam will _____ Pete at the store.

meat   meet

3. Stan fed the _____ in the park.

deer   dear

4. Eve likes the rides at the _____.

fair   fare

**Word Study**

secret
seashell
seashore

_____

_____

scares
squares
squirts

_____

_____

_____

Decoding

Sounds and Spellings

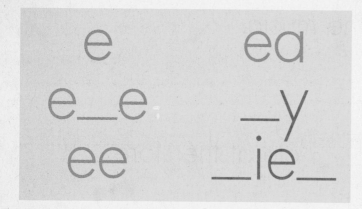

Writing Words and Sentences

chief _____  shiny _____

pony _____  ponies _____

Betty saves her pennies.

_____

Sally fed the bunnies.

_____

Name

## Reading and Writing

The lily is white.

The lilies are white.

The box is shiny.

The box is dirty.

## Dictation and Spelling

*Phonics*

Decoding/Spelling

## Writing Synonyms

| tiny | funny | muddy | unhappy |

dirty _____     silly _____

little _____     sad _____

## Listening for Words

- ○ water
- ○ winter
- ○ whisper

- ○ grass
- ○ glass
- ○ grab

- ○ story
- ○ stories
- ○ study

- ○ dirty
- ○ dizzy
- ○ distance

- ○ quack
- ○ quake
- ○ quick

- ○ sheep
- ○ shore
- ○ shape

**Word Study**

| ponies | thirsty | twenty |
| emergency | stories | cherries |

1. Popcorn can make you _____.

2. Call 911 in an _____.

3. Jerry likes to eat red _____.

4. Thirty is more than _____.

5. The _____ were nice to ride.

6. There are many _____

   to read in the library.

*Decoding*

## Sounds and Spellings

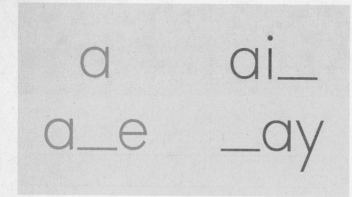

a        ai__

a__e      __ay

## Writing Words and Sentences

pail _____        snail _____

pay _____        stay _____

The raisins are stale.

_____

_____

Kay's birthday is in May.

_____

_____

## Homophones

pale   pail

_____

_____

_____

sail   sale

_____

_____

_____

tale   tail

_____

_____

_____

## Dictation and Spelling

_____    _____

_____    _____

_____    _____

_____    _____

_____    _____

_____    _____

_____    _____

_____    _____

_____    _____

Decoding/Spelling

Sounds and Spellings

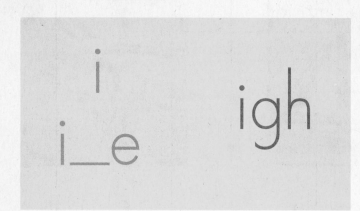

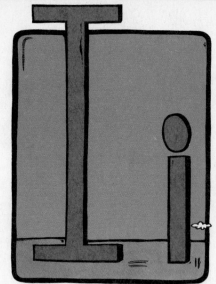

Writing Words and Sentences

high _____     sigh _____

sight _____    flight _____

The light is bright.

_____

_____

You might be right.

_____

_____

Vowel Sounds and Spellings

*Phonics*

## Writing Compound Words

| light | light |
|-------|-------|
| night | chair |
| high  | rope  |
| tight | bulb  |

_____

_____

_____

_____

_____

## Completing Sentences

_____

1. The baby eats in the _____.

_____

2. I saw a _____ walker.

_____

3. The lamp needs a _____.

_____

4. Ben sleeps with a _____.

Blending

# Name

## Sounds and Spellings

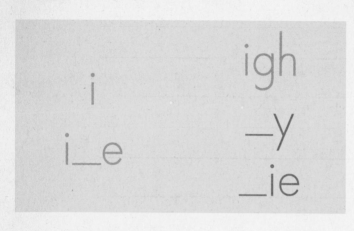

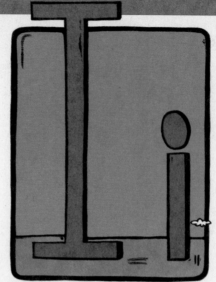

## Writing Words and Sentences

try              tries

fly              flies

The kite flies in the sky.

Try the apple pie.

| fly | tie | tries | pie | sky |

1. The _____ buzzes by my head.

2. I ate the cherry _____ all by myself.

3. Tyrone _____ to do a trick.

**Dictation and Spelling**

_____    _____

_____    _____

_____    _____

_____    _____

_____

_____

Sounds and Spellings

 ng

Writing Words and Sentences

wing _____     thing _____

ring _____     spring _____

The king rang a gong.

We sang a long song.

# Name

### Reading and Writing

 The string is tangled.

The string is in a box.

_____

_____

 Hank plays ping pong.

Hank plays the tape.

_____

_____

### Listening for Words

| | | |
|---|---|---|
| ○ hung | ○ skunk | ○ string |
| ○ hang | ○ snake | ○ strong |
| ○ hinge | ○ snap | ○ stripe |

| | | |
|---|---|---|
| ○ seed | ○ more | ○ cry |
| ○ sing | ○ mole | ○ cries |
| ○ sweet | ○ most | ○ cried |

*Phonics*

*Decoding*

**Rhyming Words**

hop     jump     sing     run     think

smile     dig     hope     hide     eat

ring _____    fig _____

feet _____    fun _____

mop _____    soap _____

bump _____    ride _____

file _____    sink _____

## Completing Sentences

1. Melissa is _____.

2. A dog is _____.

3. Sam is _____.

4. The girl is _____.

## Dictation and Spelling

_____  _____

_____  _____

_____  _____

_____  _____

_____

_____

_____

_____

Name

Completing Sentences

1. I _____ I'll play a tape.

   think   thing

2. Fred put on his _____.

   soaks   socks

3. That's a big _____ of paper.

   stack   stake

4. This is a _____ cat.

   cut   cute

5. We _____ with the music.

   sing   song

6. Tom has _____ feet.

   muddy   many

*Phonics*

Adding -ed and -ing

paint _____ _____

bake _____ _____

slip _____ _____

rule _____ _____

Writing Synonyms

song    nice    road    cute

pretty _____    kind _____

music _____    highway _____

Spelling/Decoding

Name _____

Sounds and Spellings

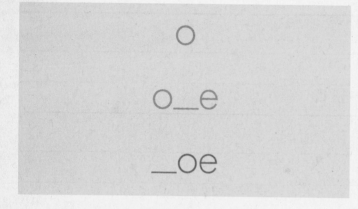

o

o__e

__oe

## Writing Words and Sentences

doe _____        tiptoe _____

Joe hit his toe with a hoe.

_____

_____

_____

## Dictation and Spelling

_____    _____    _____

_____    _____    _____

_____    _____    _____

_____    _____    _____

_____    _____    _____

Vowel Sounds and Spellings

132 R/WC

Name

## Sounds and Spellings

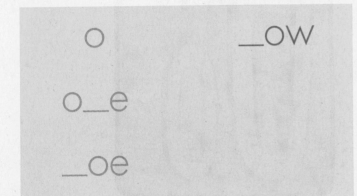

| o | _ow |
| o_e | |
| _oe | |

## Writing Words and Sentences

grow _____

throw _____

shadow _____

yellow _____

The snow blows slowly past the window.

_____

_____

_____

_____

Vowel Sounds and Spellings

Sounds and Spellings

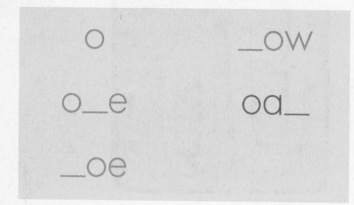

o       _ow

o_e       oa_

_oe

Writing Words and Sentences

soap _____

toast _____

A toad sat on the boat.

_____

_____

Dictation and Spelling

Vowel Sounds and Spellings

*Phonics*

Name _____

Sounds and Spellings

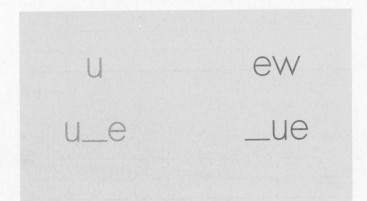

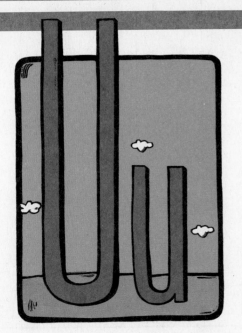

u          ew

u_e        _ue

Writing Words and Sentences

few  _____      cue  _____

chew _____      hue  _____

The fire fighter rescued the cat.

_____

_____

Vowel Sounds and Spellings

*Phonics*                                    R/WC 135

**Lesson 75**

**Writing Sentences**

1. What can you do like a deer?

_____

_____

2. What can you do like a snake?

_____

_____

3. What can you do like a tiger?

_____

_____

4. What can you do like a toad?

_____

_____

**Dictation and Spelling**

_____  _____  _____

_____  _____  _____

_____  _____  _____

_____  _____  _____

_____

_____

_____

Vowel Sounds and Spellings

Copyright © 1995 Open Court Publishing Company

*Phonics*

Sounds and Spellings

ow

Writing Words and Sentences

how _____    _____

_____    down _____

Here is a towel for your shower.

_____

_____

A cow that was <u>brown</u> went to the _____.

The queen had a <u>crown</u> and a long green _____.

I will plant a <u>flower</u> at the top of the _____.

Sounds and Spellings

OW

ou_

Writing Words and Sentences

shout _____     house _____

The little mouse made a loud sound.

_____

_____

Dictation and Spelling

_____   _____   _____

_____   _____   _____

_____   _____   _____

_____   _____   _____

_____   _____   _____

_____   _____   _____

_____   _____   _____

Vowel Sounds and Spellings

*Phonics*

| how | sound | snow | crow | crown | show |

1. The queen has a _____ with a big round ruby.

2. Do you know _____ to play checkers?

3. The class put on a puppet _____ .

4. The balloon made a loud _____ when it popped.

5. The _____ made the ground white.

6. A _____ is a big, black bird.

Vowel Sounds and Spellings

**Reading and Writing**

| outside | down | around | counts |
| --- | --- | --- | --- |
| shout | found | out | |

We play hide and seek _____.

"Not It!" Rose and I _____.

Steve is It. He _____ to ten. Rose hides under

the picnic table. I hide behind a tree. Steve hunts _____

the yard. I feel a tug _____ on my sneaker. It's my pup.

"Cut that _____," I say.

It's too late. Steve has _____ me. Now I'm It.

**Dictation and Spelling**

_____   _____   _____

_____   _____   _____

_____   _____   _____

_____   _____   _____

_____   _____   _____

_____   _____   _____

_____   _____   _____

Vowel Sounds and Spellings

Writing Words

1. The dog sleeps in the doghouse.

2. The lightbulb is burned out.

3. A stoplight is red.

4. Mother has a new keychain.

5. Jack played in the backyard.

Dictation and Spelling

Decoding/Spelling

Lesson 81

Writing Words

tall

soft

big

wide

fast

thin

grouchy

brave

Making Comparisons

*Phonics*

Name _____

Sounds and Spellings

aw

au

Writing Words and Sentences

straw _____

pause _____

The baby crawls on the lawn.

_____
_____
_____

Dictation and Spelling

_____   _____   _____
_____   _____   _____
_____   _____   _____
_____   _____   _____
_____   _____   _____
_____

Vowel Sounds and Spellings

1. The dog's _____ got dirty in the mud.

           paws   walk

2. The cat's milk is in the _____ .

           saw   saucer

3. _____ is the month after July.

    Auto   August

4. Lightning _____ the forest fire.

    called   caused

5. The _____ man juggled three _____ .

    saw   tall                    balls   shawl

6. The _____ has long _____ .

    hall   hawk             chalk   claws

Vowel Sounds and Spellings

*Phonics*

Name _____

Sounds and Spellings

oo        u_e

_ue       ew

u

Writing Words and Sentences

food  _____          flute  _____

glue  _____          jewel  _____

judo  _____          blue  _____

The balloon floats up to the moon.

_____

_____

_____

Stu plays a new tune on his tuba.

_____

_____

_____

_____

_____

Vowel Sounds and Spellings

## Writing Words

1. He huffed and he puffed and he blew the house down.

2. The farmer's goose honked at me.

3. I saw a cocoon on a leaf.

4. She made a house for bluebirds.

5. Do you know the rules of the game?

## Dictation and Spelling

Vowel Sounds and Spellings

*Phonics*

Copyright © 1995 Open Court Publishing Company

Sounds and Spellings

OO

Writing Words and Sentences

brook _____     hood _____

cook _____     wool _____

The woodpecker shook his foot.

_____

_____

She took a look at the book.

_____

_____

Vowel Sounds and Spellings

Name



Sounds and Spellings

n

**kn___**

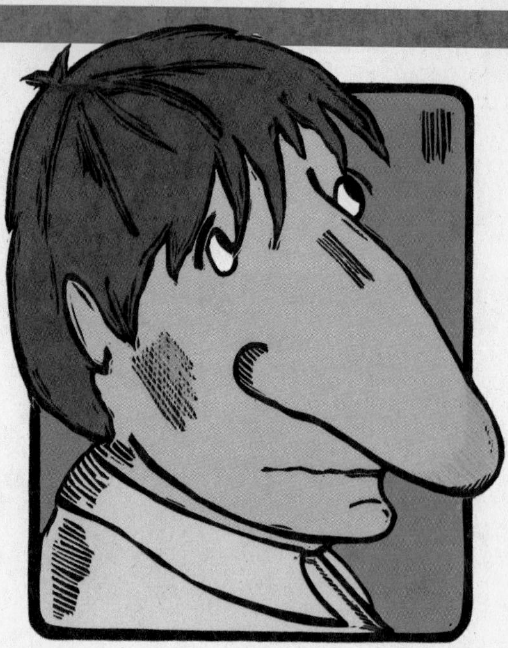

Writing Words and Sentences

knit

knot

The knight knocked on the door.

Dictation and Spelling

**Reading and Writing**

## Brad Cooks

It was almost noon. Brad wanted to cook. He took out a cookbook. He used a big spoon to make the batter smooth. Then he put his cookies in the oven. Brad used a broom to sweep up his mess. He shook his apron. When the cookies were done, he let them cool.

Vowel Sounds and Spellings

## Sounds and Spellings

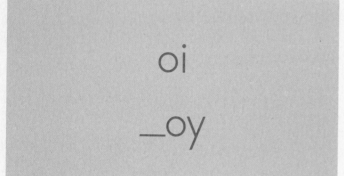

oi

_oy

## Writing Words and Sentences

noise _____        enjoy _____

The boy has a nice voice.

_____

_____

## Dictation and Spelling

_____  _____  _____

_____  _____  _____

_____  _____  _____

_____

_____

Name

Reading and Writing

1. Dolls, yo-yos, and chickens are toys. _____

2. Noodles, crayons, and cookies are food. _____

3. Root, trunk, and hook are parts of a tree. _____

4. Five, foot, and elbow are body parts. _____

5. A goose, boot, and balloon can fly. _____

6. Oil, dimes, and pennies are coins. _____

7. Foil, boil, and bake are ways to cook. _____

8. A baboon, moose, and book are animals. _____

Vowel Sounds and Spellings

## Writing Words and Sentences

gnaw

gnat

sign

design

The old tree was gnarled.

Stop at the sign.

## Dictation and Spelling

Consonant Sounds and Spellings

**Reading and Writing**

1. Jeff played with colored _____ .

                mumbles

                marbles

2. The _____ moved slowly.

                turtle

                rattle

3. _____ are hot and rainy.

                Jingles

                Jungles

4. The mouse _____ the lion's tummy.

                tickled

                tackled

5. Funny shows make me _____ .

                grumble

                chuckle

6. The green _____ was salty.

                purple

                pickle

Consonant Sounds and Spellings

**Reading and Writing**

1. The singer's voice was _____ .

loud
loudly

2. Ken's knapsack was _____ .

heavy
heavily

3. The dog gnawed the bone _____ .

noise
noisily

4. The fudge was _____ .

sweet
sweetly

**Dictation and Spelling**

_____  _____  _____

_____  _____  _____

_____  _____  _____

_____  _____  _____

_____

_____

_____

**Reading and Writing**

## Gerry the Gardener

Gerry likes to work in the garden just behind her cottage. She grows many things like green beans and cabbage. She has the biggest carrots in town. Gerry likes to give her pals Ginger, Gail, and Jack the things she grows in her garden.

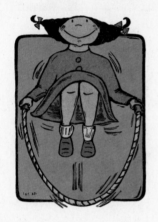

_____

_____

_____

_____

_____

_____

_____

_____

_____

Consonant Sounds and Spellings

Lesson 95

Sounds and Spellings

r

**wr__**

Writing Words and Sentences

wrist

wrap

A robot wrestles wriggly snakes.

Dictation and Spelling

Consonant Sounds and Spellings

*Phonics*

Name

Sounds and Spellings

f
ph

Writing Words and Sentences

photo _____          gopher _____

phone _____          elephant _____

trophy _____          dolphin _____

Phil's nephew plays the saxophone.

_____

_____

_____

_____

Consonant Sounds and Spellings

Name _____

**Reading and Writing**

1. Squares, circles, and snakes are shapes.    _____

2. Birds, children, and cats can sing.    _____

3. Tennis, daisy, and soccer are sports.    _____

4. Cars, rulers, and girls have feet.    _____

5. Sandals, books, and sneakers are shoes.    _____

**Dictation and Spelling**

_____    _____    _____

_____    _____    _____

_____    _____    _____

_____

_____

_____

*Phonics*

**Reading and Writing**

1. The elephant was huge.

2. A plane was high in the sky.

3. Did Dad read the mail?

4. The day was cold.

5. Will Pat go to the store?

6. Pete has an ice cube.

7. The sheep are cute.

_____

_____

_____

_____

_____

_____

_____

_____

_____

_____

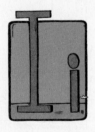

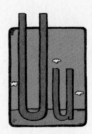

_____

_____

_____

_____

_____

_____

_____

_____

_____

_____

_____

_____

Vowel Sounds and Spellings

_Phonics_

**Lesson 99**

**Reading and Writing**

1. Horses, chairs, and snakes have legs. _____

2. Robins, eagles, and lizards have feathers. _____

3. Bread, tubas, and sandwiches are food. _____

4. Phones, alarm clocks, and pigs can ring. _____

5. Ropes, buckets, and sneakers can be tied. _____

**Dictation and Spelling**

Decoding and Spelling

Copyright © 1995 Open Court Publishing Company

*Phonics*

**Reading and Writing**

| smile | dress | spilled | spend | money | lay |

A girl had a pail of milk to sell. She had the pail on her head.

As she was walking along, she began to plan.

"The man will give me _____ for this milk.

I will _____ the money for a hen. The hen will

_____ eggs. Then I can sell the eggs."

"Soon I will have money for a fine new _____.

Farmer Tom will smile at me. I will _____ right back

and nod my head, just like this."

When the girl nodded her head, the pail fell off. The milk

_____ on the ground.

What did the girl learn? _____

_____

_____

Using Story Context

**Reading and Writing**

"May I have some watermelon?"

_____

_____ Wally.

asked    answered

"Yes," Mother answered, "but first

_____

_____ your hands."

wash    watch

Wally stood on a _____ and washed with soap and

box    wax

_____ water. Mother _____ a slice of

wart    warm                                    cute    cut

watermelon for him.

Wally nibbled the red melon. He _____ to see

checked    clicked

if Mother was looking, then he _____ a melon seed

tugged    tossed

into the _____. He hoped the seed would become a

hedge    help

_____ that would grow more melons.

plan    plant

Listening for Vowel Sounds

The sun shines on the jungle. It makes patches of shade and light. A tiger sits in the shadows. Her coat is gold like the sun's light. It has stripes of black like the shade. The tiger blends in with her jungle home.

Phonics Review

Completing Sentences

When Wilma Rudolph was a little girl, she had polio.

The doctor was _____ she would not be

_____

_____ to walk again. He told her to exercise
after    afraid

_____

to _____ her legs stronger. At first, walking
apple    able

make    may

was painful but Wilma was a _____ girl. She got

bat    brave

stronger and stronger. Soon she began to run.

She became a very good _____.

runner    ranger

She won many _____. In 1960, she ran at the

races    rackets

Olympic _____ and won three gold medals!

gates    games

*Phonics*

Name _____

**Completing Sentences**

1. Dogs like to chew _____.

   soap    bones    bottles

2. You can open _____.

   rocks    goats    windows

3. Arthur crossed the lake in a _____.

   boat    home    crow

4. The _____ ate hay and oats.

   phone    pony    rainbow

5. Joan tells funny _____.

   jokes    jobs    toads

6. When I am cold I put on my _____.

   rope    coat    cot

7. Stan called his mom on the _____.

   toast    phone    colt

8. Frank spilled his _____.

   corner    elbow    cocoa

**Finishing Letters**

_____
_____ Grandma Bea,
Dear    Bread

Thank you for the birthday gifts. I had hoped all _____
year    yield

that I would get a kite. I'll fly it in the _____ high over
measure    meadow

my _____. Thanks for the red _____,
head    hear                                sweeter    sweater

too. I _____ like it!
really    ready

Love, Peter

Dear Peter,

Thanks for the letter. Yesterday I _____ to see
stopping    stopped

Uncle Hank. I _____ him with his boat. We
helped    helping

_____ the deck and _____ the sides.
mopping    mopped                    painted    painting

Then we went for a boat _____.
ride    riding

Love, Grandma Bea

Listening For Vowel Sounds

It was lunch time. Huey was hungry. He looked at a menu and ordered a huge sandwich. Huey had fun as he waited for his lunch. He watched a lady amuse her baby with a fuzzy toy. He saw a boy argue with his sister. A few pups jumped up and down outside. At last Huey got his sandwich. He chewed it happily.

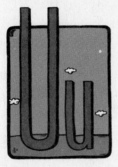

_____
_____
_____
_____
_____
_____
_____
_____
_____
_____
_____
_____

Phonics Review

**Reading**

1.  Which cannot fly?

    ____ a balloon

    ____ a raccoon

    ____ a goose

2.  Which keeps you warm?

    ____ a queen

    ____ a quilt

    ____ a square

3.  Which is makes you cool?

    ____ a pool

    ____ a stew

    ____ a spoon

4.  Which is stickiest?

    ____ shampoo

    ____ tuna

    ____ glue

5.  Which is hardest?

    ____ a squash

    ____ a noodle

    ____ a tooth

6.  Which is highest?

    ____ the moon

    ____ a roof

    ____ a kangaroo

7.  Which is most quiet?

    ____ a quack

    ____ a squeal

    ____ a whisper

8.  Which is tool?

    ____ a stool

    ____ a flute

    ____ a screwdriver

9.  What can you eat?

    ____ a new tool

    ____ a blue jewel

    ____ a tuna sandwich

*Phonics*

Listening for Vowel Sounds

"What do you like about parades?" asked Mom.

"I like the sound of drums," said Byron, "but I wish they weren't so loud."

"The clowns are funny," added Suzy. "One of them was walking slow and made our dog growl."

"I like to see the crowd wave and clap," said Dad.

"I know what I like," said Mom. "I like to hear the bands beat their drums and blow their horns."

ou

ow

ow

_____

_____

_____

_____

_____

_____

Phonics Review

**Reading**

1. Which sounds most like a thunderstorm?

____ a quiet piano

____ an old radio

____ a loud drum

2. Which looks most like a jack-o-lantern?

____ an orange peel

____ a hollow pumpkin

____ corn on the cob

3. Which feels most like a spider web?

____ cotton candy

____ a long rope

____ a wool blanket

4. Which sounds most like a hoot owl?

____ a lion

____ a tuba

____ a wooden flute

5. Which is the blowing wind?

____ a snow storm

____ a cold breeze

____ a rain shower

6. Which flaps its wings like a bat?

____ an owl

____ a balloon

____ an airplane

7. Which looks most like a full moon?

____ a spool of thread

____ a smoky fire

____ a smooth plate

Phonics Review

**Completing Sentences**

"Time _____ bed," Mother said. Frank hugged his

for    fold

dog Spunky. He did not _____ bed was a good idea.

thing    think

He was afraid of the dark.

"We're not _____," Frank said. Mother pointed to the

tired    timer

_____. Frank went to his room and got into bed. He pulled

stairs    states

his blanket up to his _____. Suddenly he felt something

north    nose

_____ on his foot.

cold    corn

"A monster is getting me!" Frank yelled. Mother _____

tuned    turned

on the light. There was Spunky, licking Frank's foot.

Phonics Review

**Listening for Vowel Sounds**

## Camp Out

Last week I camped out
with my friend Audrey. We put
up the tent on my front lawn.
Audrey brought the pillows and crawled in first. I hauled
the sleeping bags from the house. Audrey caught a
firefly, and we put it in a jar. I taught her a song.
Then we told spooky stories until we began to
yawn. We thought we should go to sleep since it would
soon be dawn. Suddenly, we saw a paw outside the tent!

_____   _____   _____
_____   _____   _____
_____   _____   _____
_____   _____   _____
_____   _____   _____
_____   _____   _____
_____   _____   _____

What do you think was outside the tent?

_____
_____
_____
_____

Completing Sentences

Our trip to the city was _____. The
exciting    exit

bus drove over a big _____. We looked
fudge    bridge

up at _____ skyscrapers. Midge was
giant    jungle

amazed at how _____ they were. We found a
huge    edge

quiet _____ to eat. It was in the _____
palace    place                                center    counter

of a park. George shared a _____ of his
slice    slick

apple. I spent fifty _____ for popcorn. I will
cents    carrots

write about this trip on a _____ of my notebook.
page    piggle

*Phonics*

**Completing Sentences**

Uncle Fred gave Roy a pile of _____ to spend
1
canes   coins

at the store. Like any _____, Roy wants to make a
2
bowl   boy

wise _____. All he really wants is something to
choice   chance   3

help him sleep. He has been grouchy and hardly
4                                              5

_____ anything lately. His sleep has been
enjoys   engines   6

_____ by a _____ in the night.
spilled   spoiled           nose   noise   7

The branches outside his bedroom window sound like

somebody tapping. Giant shadows look like _____.
8                                              oysters   monsters

"I see what I need!" Roy said in a loud _____.
vote   voice

He _____ at what he wanted. Uncle Fred reached up
9   painted   pointed

for it, then handed Roy a
10

| | | | | | | | | | |
|---|---|---|---|---|---|---|---|---|---|
| 1 | 2 | 3 | 4 | 5 | 6 | 7 | 8 | 9 | 10 |

Completing Sentences

1. The pig is _____. His tail is _____.

                thirty   dirty                    curly   early

2. The _____ is a funny looking _____.

         turkey   perky                  third   bird

3. People _____ money when they _____.

        earn   burn                  worm   work

4. _____ to be _____ in line.

   Worry   Hurry          first   burst

5. _____ the cake batter until it is smooth.

   Stir   Fur

Then bake it until you are _____ it is done.

                      concert   certain

6. I am _____ for your house.

      searching   perching

Should I _____ right or left?

     turn   churn

Phonics Review

### Reading for Information

The Sioux people carried tepees with them when they hunted. Families used vegetables and berries to make paint. They painted pictures on their <u>tepee</u>. The pictures told about their lives. Tepees are made of wood poles and bark. They are shaped like cones.

Seminole people live in Florida. Long ago their homes had open sides because the weather was very warm. The roof was made of palm leaves. A <u>chickee</u> was built on a platform. Seminoles often slept in comfortable hammocks.

Many Iroquois families shared the same home. Twenty families could live in one long, narrow house. Each family had its own fire. Sharing the <u>longhouse</u> helped the people stay warm in the terrible, northern winters.

_____    _____    _____

_____    _____    _____

**Completing Sentences**

Dear Uncle Phil,

I like our new house. It has been _____ watching

fun    phone

the workers. The plumber has a big _____ to

ranch    wrench

_____ the pipes. The carpenter let me watch him saw.

fix    photograph

I made hand prints in the _____.

cement    excitement

I'm sending you some _____. Come visit

gophers    photos

us when the _____ are finished!

workers    wrestlers

_____ me a letter soon.

Wrinkle    Write

Your _____,

niece    nephew

Ralph

**Lesson 117**

**Completing Sentences**

| lotion | nation | station | questions | attention |
| vacation | pollution | protection | billion |

| Sunday | We're going on a _____ at a ranch. |

| Monday | It's fun riding on a train. Dad said to pay _____ _____ to the sights out the window. |

| Tuesday | We arrived at the ranch. The air smells fresh and clean. There is no _____ here. |

| Wednesday | We rode horses all day. I wore _____ and a hat for _____ from the sun. |

| Thursday | There are lots of cowhands here. I want to be one when I grow up. I asked lots of _____. |

| Friday | On the train ride home, I looked out the window. I think there were a _____ stars in the sky! |

| Saturday | We're home! Aunt Rosa met us at the _____. |

*Spelling Pattern tion, ion*

*Phonics*

## Contractions

"What's the hurry?" Max yelled.

"I'm on my way to a surprise party for Penny," I answered in a quiet voice.

"Why are you talking so softly? I can't hear you!" Max shouted.

"Because the party is a surprise. I'll tell you about it later," I replied in a quieter voice.

"I still didn't hear you," he roared.

"Max," I whispered, "Don't ask about Penny's surprise party."

"Why?" he asked loudly.

"Because!" I screamed. "She's standing right behind you!"

_____     _____ + _____

_____     _____ + _____

_____     _____ + _____

_____     _____ + _____

_____     _____ + _____

_____     _____ + _____

_____     _____ + _____

**Completing Sentences**

## Animal Coloring

_____

_____

_____ is easy for some animals. Their color

    Hide    Hiding
_____

_____ the things around them. A cottontail

  match    matches

rabbit is _____ to see in a field of brown grass.

    hard   hardly
_____

_____ fawns match the tall weeds. Often their

Spotted   Spitting

enemies are _____ to see them.

    unhappy   unable

The _____ of some animals helps them

    color   colorful

hunt. A polar bear blends in with the snow. It can sneak up on

_____

an _____ animal.

  unlucky   unlocked

Completing Sentences

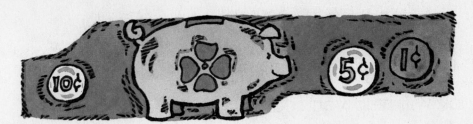

1. Dimes, nickels, and pennies are all _____.

paper    coins

2. Most rooms have four _____.

corners    doors

3. People squeeze _____ for breakfast.

oranges    corn

4. Another word for dirt is _____.

south    soil

5. When water is hot it will _____.

boil    bowl

6. A bird has a beak. A person has a _____.

month    mouth

7. _____, noon, and night are all times of day.

Moist    Morning

8. You can buy food, clothing, and furniture at a _____.

stone    store

**Listening for Vowel Sounds**

The Book Nook is my favorite store. Mr. and Mrs. Cook own the store. You can hang your coat on a hook. Then you can look for books. Mr. Cook will help you search.

Mrs. Cook tells stories at noon on Saturdays. She sits on a stool in the middle of the room. Soon children gather around. Last week she read a book about ducks that lived in a swimming pool. It was a good story!

_____ _____

_____ _____

_____ _____

_____ _____

_____ _____

_____ _____

_____

_____

Phonics Review

## Using Words with Affixes

We must be _____ at all times. This is

care    careful

very important when _____ a street. Cars and trucks

cross    crossing

can be _____. Most drivers try not to be

danger    dangerous

_____. We must remember _____ rules.

careless    care                                    safe    safety

Once my sneaker came _____ while I was

untied    retied

crossing the street. I almost tripped on the laces. That was almost an

_____ day for me!

lucky    unlucky

**Vowels Followed by R**

1. Hermit crabs, turtles, and fish have shells. _____

2. Cows, birds, and horses are heavy. _____

3. Marbles, emeralds, and pearls are jewels. _____

4. Circles, triangles, and squirms are shapes. _____

5. Parks, jungles, and classrooms have trees. _____

6. Kittens, tigers, and bears all roar. _____

7. Spiders, worms, and giraffes are little. _____

8. Bats, balls, and rakes are for playing. _____

9. Claws, crayons, and markers are for drawing. _____

10. Biking, swimming, and flying are ways to exercise. _____

*Phonics*